THE AWS PROFIT PLAYBOOK

THE AWS PROFIT PLAYBOOK

ADITYA AGARWAL

Available on amazonkindle

Worldwide Published by

Pendown Press
PREMIUM BUSINESS PUBLISHER

PENDOWN PRESS LLP

An ISO 9001 & ISO 14001 Certified Co.,

Regd. Office: 3767A, Kanhaiya Nagar,

Tri Nagar, Delhi-110035

Ph.: 8130886000, 9650072927

E-mail: info@pendownpress.com

Branch Office: 1A/2A, 20, Hari Sadan, Ansari Road,

Daryaganj, New Delhi-110002

Ph.: 011-45794768

Website: PendownPress.com

Edition: 2026

Price: ₹ 499

ISBN: 978-93-7217-871-5

Layout and Cover Designed by Pendown Graphics Team

Dedicated To,

My daughter Anvi.

You are the light of my life and make me look forward to every single day with new enthusiasm, energy, and gratitude.

Table of Contents

Acknowledgements

My parents

For being the solid pillar to my success, allowing me to take bold decisions, fall, rise, and correct myself. And to always teach me to be humble, and grounded, be it any circumstance

My wife

For all the support, even when I was at my lowest. For always believing I was built for greatness. And for your unconditional love.

I love you.

My Joint Family

For the invaluable and infinite childhood memories filled with love from all corners. I had the best upbringing one can hope for.

CHAPTER 1

Introduction: The Cloud Expense Trap

Hello, I'm **Aditya**, a.k.a. The Cloud Guy, and welcome to *The AWS Profit Playbook.*

I've spent the last decade working with companies, large and small, as a ***software architect*** designing custom software and complex workflows, not saving on cloud costs. So, the next logical question is.

Why does a software architect write a book on AWS Cost Saving?

Before I answer this question, I want to tell you that I have helped people save ***over 3 million dollars*** last year in recurring AWS Costs for my clients, which was also my first year doing it.

I did it by:

- Analysing patterns
- Optimising resource utilisation
- Dockerizing stuff when needed
- Or simply by changing some money eating configurations in their AWS Account.

I have worked with startups having cloud costs from 2000$ a month to large businesses having bills up to 300,000$ a month.

I have **saved from 20% - 85% costs for different companies** and have gathered a decent user base in the last year.

So, again, *why this book?*

I was a happy software architect for the past decade, designing optimal software solutions for my clients, which took care of performance and scalability, but was very little focused on costs, since it was the last thing I was worried about.

It was a cozy evening last to last (2023) September, when my very dear friend Arun, who had returned to India from San Francisco, came to meet me in my apartment in Bangalore for dinner.

He had recently come back to India 6 months back to start his fintech venture with a fair amount of capital he had built during his US tenure. He came here along with his wife and 3-year-old son.

Everything seemed fine until dinner, before we went for a night stroll.

When conversations got deeper, he revealed that he was almost **broke**.

What? Arun? Broke? He was one of the smartest people I knew.

He shared how he had built his business and shifted from one cloud provider to another in the past 12 months or so, and had exhausted a combined credit of over 1,50,000 USD from various cloud providers, **and now all his profits were going to cover his cloud costs once the credits were over.**

He had not even started earning a decent revenue in his startup yet, **but his cloud costs were *spiralling out of control.***

I could see the helplessness in his eyes and the fear of what would happen next to his startup, his personal life, and how he would reveal this to his wife, who had so much confidence in him, and his kid, who called *Papa* a thousand times a day.

The incident shook me, and when I googled this later in the night, I saw numerous startups juggling with this exact same problem every day, worried about how to survive another month with their cloud costs.

I called more of my startup friends, and came across a ***shocking figure***.

Cloud Costs were the single highest expense in their business, ranging from 20% to 45% of their revenue. Even for businesses running for 10+ years.

This looks like a decent expense in revenue terms, but in terms of profit, it is *mind-boggling*.

For a startup with a **net profit of 10%,** you can **DOUBLE** your profit **just by saving 25% on your cloud costs**. And it does.

I'll explain this in more detail in the next chapter.

For a startup running at a loss, it could mean the difference between *failure and survival.*

Coming back to the point, this incident with Arun kick-started my journey into Cloud Optimization.

I had worked mostly with Amazon Cloud, which I loved, and took an oath to create a business to optimise cloud costs for every business I could help in my capacity.

This oath turned into a passion, and one after another, **we transformed 50+ businesses last year to profit-making machines out of thin air.**

This book is a culmination of:

- The lessons I learned
- The patterns I saw
- The mistakes that you, I, and every entrepreneur make to fall into the cloud expense trap
- And how can we make small, but steady improvements to come out of this trap and turn our cloud into a **profit centre**?

The influx of easy credit from cloud providers leads to misuse of resources, low optimization for startups, who want to quickly get to market.

They focus less on their cloud costs, and by the time they realise, their costs have reached a whopping $2000-$5000 a month, and they are not yet profitable enough to sustain that cost, maintain their expensive team, and get new business, all at once.

This, my friend, I call the Cloud Expense Trap.

This book is my effort to show you exactly how to achieve drastically lower cloud costs *without* cutting corners on performance or reliability.

The principles in the book apply to all cloud providers, not only AWS, but the terminology I use may be specific to AWS Services since it's the highest share of my clients, though I try my best to be vendor agnostic.

Who Can Benefit From This Book?

This book is written for those tech founders who feel unsure about how optimized their cloud deployment is.

You might be technical, might not be, but this book will help you to analyse step-by-step what's not working in your cloud and also help you to guide your team to fix it for better scalability, higher security, and ***way less costs.***

You may be paying just under 1000$ today in your cloud costs, or you may be paying 10x, 20x more, but the principles apply to you nevertheless.

You **DO NOT need to be technical** to read this book.

You just need an open, *curious* mind.

So, let's dive in!

CHAPTER 2

Why Should You Even Focus on AWS Cost?

To some people, AWS costs might seem like a simple budgeting line item. But the truth is, uncontrolled AWS bills are often a **symptom** of deeper issues, such as:

- Sloppy code and architecture.
- Fear-driven over-provisioning.
- Poor or non-existent lifecycle policies for data and logs.
- Untested processes that lead to accidental "leaks" in the form of idle resources.

When your AWS bill balloons beyond reason, *it's rarely just about money;* it reveals the gaps in your overall software development and operational practices.

It is like a tumour which you know you have, but you fail to address and is growing into cancer day by day.

If you're sceptical that it's such a deep issue, keep on reading the next few chapters. By the time we circle back here, you'll have a new appreciation for how cost management also boosts *performance, agility, and security.*

Also, let's talk a little bit more in detail about the money involved.

If you own a tech company, today or tomorrow, your tech costs will **go from 20 to 60% of your net revenue**.

Not profit.

Revenue.

20% revenue can be 100% more profit.

You don't believe me.

So here is a study with a source cited of some of the top companies you are already aware of. Look at the chart.

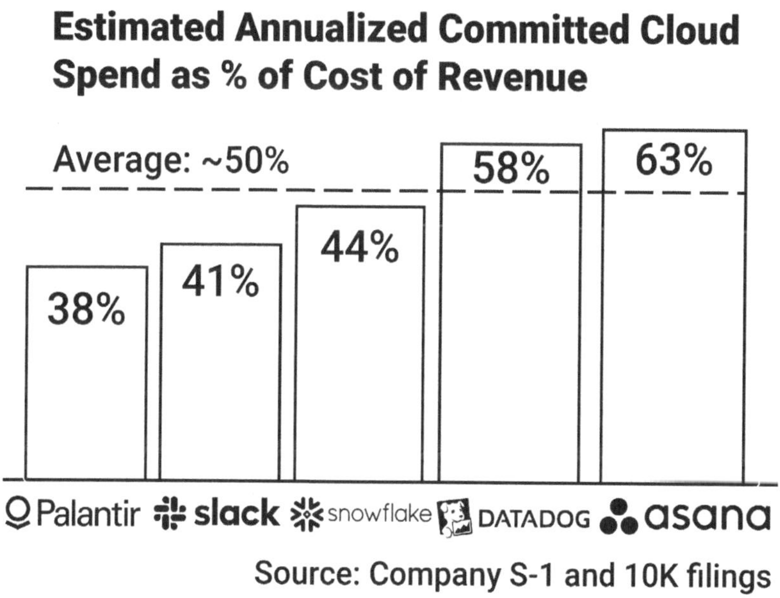

Stats Credits: a16z.com

The story is the **same from small to big companies.**

Some can survive this due to their sales volume. But the easiest way for a tech company to have exponentially more profit is to optimize its cloud to extract maximum potential.

Shocked? Let's look at one more graph to understand how efficiently we use our Cloud resources.

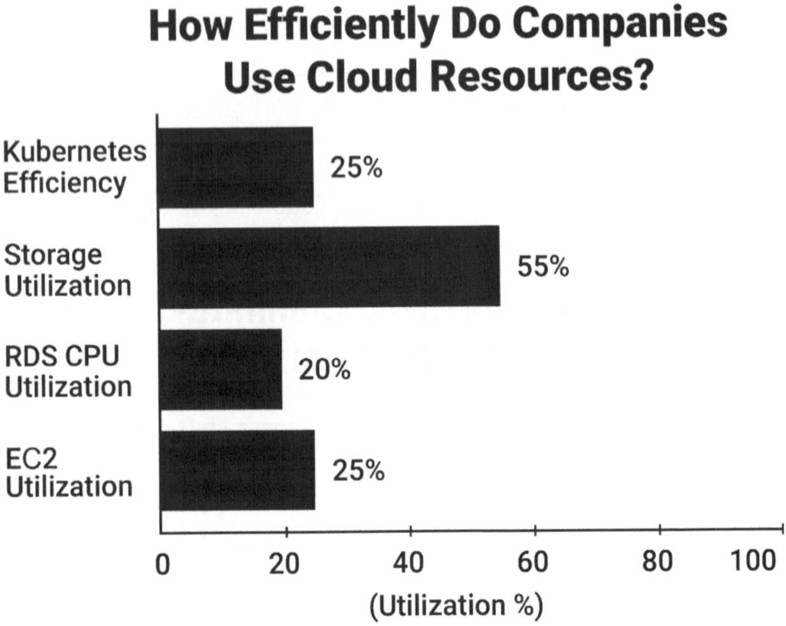

Credits: FinOps Foundation State of FinOps 2023; Dropbox S-1 2018; Basecamp Blog 2022; Cast.ai case studies. Chart recreated by Aditya using public data.

A typical company wastes from 50-70% of its cloud resources. The figure may be much higher for you.

CHAPTER 3

Common Myths About AWS Costs

Myth 1: "AWS is too expensive. Other providers are cheaper." Reality: AWS charges hourly, not monthly. While the hourly rates are higher in one-to-one comparison with cheaper providers, the overall beauty lies in how you can adjust your system to use the resources you use, which makes you agile, cheap, and fast.

A simple comparison for a VPS is this:

An 8 vCPU,32 GB RAM VPS Cost Analysis.

Provider	**Monthly Cost** (Approx)	**Hourly Cost**
Digital Ocean	$250	0.35
Linode/Vultr	**$200**	0.27
AWS/ GCP/ Azure	$300	0.48

**AWS Charges are not straightforward; I have taken the higher side of a typical use case.*

So, let's assume we have a magic wand, and we reduce the AWS Server to work at 50% capacity for 50% of the time it runs every day (non-peak hours).

Now, the SAME cost chart changes like this :

Provider	**Monthly Cost (Approx)**
Digital Ocean	$250
Linode/Vultr	$200
AWS/GCP/Aziure	$300 / 2 + $150/2 = **$225**

Also, this AWS has component-based pricing.

Need more space? No need to upgrade your RAM and CPU too unlike other VPS Systems.

Myth 2: "Performance will tank if I reduce costs."

Reality: In the majority of AWS environments, 70% or more of the costs come from resources that do **nothing** for performance. They're just leftover by-products of hasty decisions or fear-based over-provisioning.

Surprisingly, really focusing on optimization tends to ***improve*** performance because it forces you to streamline code, architecture, and overall system design.

Myth 3: "No single person has a complete picture of my software, so we risk breaking our software by adjusting resources."

Reality: Lack of visibility is not an AWS problem—it's an organizational problem. The moment you adopt better cost and resource tracking, you start establishing better internal processes, improving documentation, and bridging knowledge gaps. That *prevents* breakage and promotes self-healing, self-scaling deployment practices.

Myth 4: "Some AI tool can magically analyse and solve my AWS costs."

Reality: AWS cost optimization is part art, part science. Tools can flag areas of improvement, but they can't factor in your team's code structure, deployment pipeline, or your business's nuances. A curious, methodical approach that involves your team is irreplaceable as of today.

Myth 5: "Changing Cloud Provider will result in Savings"

Shifting is time-intensive, expensive, and often yields little to zero net benefit if the real culprits—misuse of resources, poor design, and lack of cost-awareness—remain unaddressed.

Migrating to a different provider usually means incurring migration costs, re-architecting complexities, and the same inefficiencies carried over to the new platform, resulting in a new cost-eating demon that has a different name.

Moreover, many other providers are not able to provide the level of comfort and managed services that you are already accustomed to.

Now that we have a fair idea of the theory, let's see some easy-to-implement practical steps to break the trap. I present the steps in the manner I like to look, decipher, and solve. So, let's start with the most basic, most informative thing to start with - The AWS invoice.

Figure Out the Elephants.

The aim is to figure out where our costs are leaking. You will see that it is surprisingly easy to figure out what we need to focus on once we know the art of evaluating costs.

AWS gives a wonderful but hard-to-explore tool called **Cost Explorer** for this. We will use this to figure out what is causing the maximum usage for our bill.

I will teach you my secret, which is that more than half the work is done by checking the Cost Explorer. By the end of this chapter, you will know where to pinpoint the largest chunk of bills and where to draw our attention first.

One of our startup clients in the USA identified that they are paying 3000$ in Data Transfer Egress Charges in EC2. They changed a single service to work internally instead of over the internet, and saved over 3000$ a month, every month. ***In 5 minutes.*** This is the power of observation. So, let's start.

Here is what a typical AWS Cost Explorer Usage graph looks like. Let's see our daily cost bifurcation.

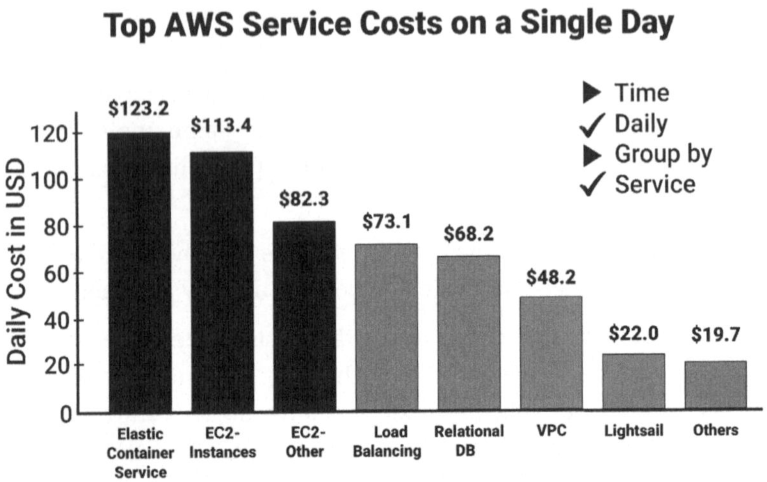

Source: AWS Cost Explorer. Visualization recreated by Aditya for educational purposes.

Step 1: Figure out the biggest cost driver service for you by checking "Daily" costs grouped by "Service".

In our above example, the highest cost drivers are **ECS, EC2, and EC2-Others.**

Step 2: For each such service, we will further break it down. To do this:

Add the service to the "Filter-> Service".

Change the group by to "Usage Type".

Breakdown of EC2 – Other by Usage Type (Daily Cost)

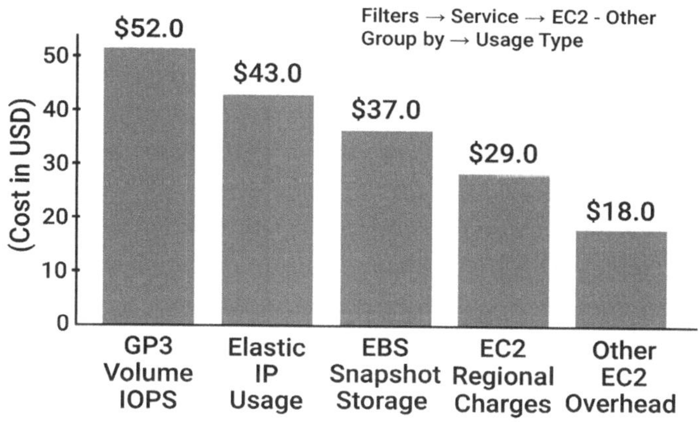

Source: AWS Cost Explorer. Visualization recreated by Aditya for educational purposes.

On doing that, we see something like this.

Which means we are paying 50$ daily for an EBS Volume, which is GP3-> IOPS.

This data, combined with the knowledge I give in the next chapters, can help us reduce our costs in a focused manner, one at a time.

Now, prepare a list of the biggest cost drivers by service, usage type, and cost. Keep the strategy column empty. We will fill this column with our reduction strategy.

Service	Usage Type	Current Cost/ day	Strategy
EC2	Box Usage t3a. medium	60	
RDS	DataTransfer-In-Bytes	50	

We have a handy Excel which you can print quickly to note this. https:// thecloudguy.ai/serviceexcel

Addressing the Elephants.

Once you know the cost drivers, you have a fair idea of what to do. I am doing a quick list-down of the strategies that can be applied to the most common driving factors you will find. We will cover the more interesting points in more detail in later chapters. If you prefer your team do the heavy lifting, you can share this list with them and skip the next pages of this chapter. I have also shared a handy link which explains this and more for your team at the end of this chapter to share with them, along with the printout.

EC2 :

Box Usage:

1. If no auto scaling, apply auto scaling. [Divide one big server into 3 mini servers, which start/stop to accommodate load based on CPU/ RAM load]
2. Apply auto shutdown startup scripts to Lambda to shut down UAT, dev servers.
3. For heavy-scheduled jobs that need a lot of CPU, spin up temporary servers, or club them to a single server with different time durations for managing optimal usage. You can use Lambda or AWS Batch for this.
4. If too many EC2s, each with high resource wastage, consider shifting to Kubernetes.

Data Transfer

See if your EC2s are connecting over the internet, instead of the intranet, amongst internal services. Figure out what data they are exporting? (incoming data is typically free). E.g., you may be uploading files to S3 via the internet, or connecting to your DB via the internet, and changing all of them to use the VPC internal network. If your team can really justify the outgoing data (which is rare in EC2), then no optimization here.

RDS

1. **Multi A-Z:** Check if you really need Multi A-Z deployment for non-critical DBs (it can 2-3x your costs)
2. **Provisioned IOPS**: See if you are using provisioned IOPS or General Purpose (GP3), and do you really need them. Most use cases can do well with a general-purpose. Provisioned IOPS are far more expensive than General Purpose.
3. **Size**: Check your DB connections, CPU, and RAM to see if you can reduce your DB size. If usage varies drastically with time (10% to 90+ %), consider a serverless Aurora deployment.

S3 (Simple Storage Service)

1. **Review storage class:** Are you using Standard for everything? Move infrequently accessed data to S3-IA, Glacier, or Glacier Deep Archive.
2. **Apply lifecycle rules:** Automatically transition objects to cheaper storage classes or delete them after a certain age.
3. **Delete old versions:** If versioning is enabled, old versions may be bloating storage.
4. **Avoid cross-region access:** Accessing S3 buckets across regions incurs transfer charges. Use region-local buckets if possible.
5. **Leverage CloudFront:** For frequently accessed assets, use CloudFront to cache and reduce S3 + transfer costs.

Overwhelmed?

Here is a link that gives the same info for sharing with your team.

https://thecloudguy.ai/common-fixes

CHAPTER 4

Don't Fear the Zombies: Control-Alt-Delete It!

One of the biggest cost drains is the *fear of deleting something important.* Over the course of development, teams spin up proof-of-concept environments, stash backups everywhere, and then leave them running out of fear that turning them off might break something. These accumulate until you're paying for a bunch of "maybes" or "just-in-cases." I see a massive fear in businesses to touch these zombie instances, files, DBs, etc. So, I carefully designed this Ctrl-Alt-Delete strategy to get rid of them risk-free.

Control-Alt-Delete Strategy

- **Control**: Identify a resource you suspect is unused.
- **Alt**: Put it to "alternate "mode (stop the instance, rename or archive the S3 object), so you have a fallback.
- **Delete**: If no one complains or notices after a defined window (e.g., 7 days), proceed to delete. Wait another 30 days for any final issues to arise. If all remains quiet, remove it permanently.

This strategy not only reduces costs but cleanses your deployment by removing clutter. During one project for a fintech client, we found **12 M-XL EC2s** running for unknown reasons. Everyone was too afraid to stop them. With a controlled approach, we systematically shut them down—and guess what? **Nothing broke.**

Those instances turned out to be left over from an old pilot project, costing thousands of dollars monthly for no reason.

CHAPTER 5

Redundant Data = Redundant Business

We all like to have data accessible at our fingertips. But does your customer *really* need to query a 6-month-old metric every day? If historical data is rarely accessed, shift it to cheaper, cold storage. Paying premium rates for data that's seldom used is akin to storing your high-school baseball trophies in a luxury penthouse apartment; you're paying for location without gaining any real benefit.

Data is often compared to oil in the digital economy. But in practice, too much unrefined, unused, and poorly stored data is less like oil and more like toxic waste; it takes up space, adds risk, and costs a fortune to store.

Think about the different types of data sitting in your AWS environment:

- **Customer Data:** Profiles, transaction histories, uploaded files.
- **System Data:** Logs, snapshots, backups.
- **Analytics Data:** Clickstreams, tracking events, A/B testing results.

The problem? Most startups treat all of this data the same, store it on S3 Standard, keep all versions forever, and pay the bill every month without asking:

Do we really need this?

Practical Steps:

1. **Tiered Storage:**
   - Move old data from S3 Standard to cheaper classes like S3-IA (Infrequent Access) or Glacier.
   - Example: An edtech client reduced their S3 costs by **70%** just by pushing old student activity logs to Glacier Deep Archive.
2. **Data Lifecycle Policies:** Automate deletion or archiving of data beyond a certain age. Most businesses don't need to keep *raw clickstream data* beyond 90 days—summarize it, extract insights, and delete the raw logs.
3. **Backups & Snapshots:**
   - Do you really need daily RDS snapshots for 365 days? Probably not.
   - Keep hourly/daily for the last week, weekly for the last month, and monthly for long-term compliance.
4. **Data Minimization for Compliance:** Keeping unnecessary customer data isn't just costly—it's risky under GDPR/CCPA.

A Real-World Example

A fintech startup I worked with had **14 TB of old transactional data** in S3 Standard. Upon review, we found 80% of it hadn't been accessed in 2+ years. By shifting it to Glacier and deleting redundant versions, they saved **$3,000 a year**.

The takeaway: Redundant data doesn't just hurt your AWS bill; it slows you down, increases risk, and clutters your business intelligence.

Lean data = lean business.

CHAPTER 6

Logs: A Mountain of Them!

Logs are critical for debugging and audit trails, but they grow faster than weeds in a summer garden. Many companies have no lifecycle policy, so logs just pile up indefinitely. A simple policy, such as automatically archiving logs older than 30 days to a cheaper storage tier, can save a fortune.

Logs are essential, until they aren't. **They're like receipts: useful when reconciling, but absurd to keep forever.**

Startups often fall into the trap of *hoarding logs forever "just in case."* Without lifecycle rules, logs keep piling up, leading to spiraling costs in S3, CloudWatch, and even Elasticsearch clusters.

Common Log Pitfalls

- **CloudWatch Retention Defaults:** CloudWatch logs have no expiration by default. That means your 2018 dev logs are still sitting there, costing you money.
- **Overly Verbose Logging:** Debug-level logs left on in production can multiply log volumes 10x.
- **Elasticsearch Addiction:** Using Elasticsearch clusters as a permanent log store is like renting a luxury condo for storing cardboard boxes.

Practical Fixes

1. **Retention Policies:** Set retention to 30 days for most services. For compliance-heavy industries, archive instead of retaining forever.

2. **Offload to S3 + Athena:** Instead of paying for Elasticsearch, move logs to S3 and query them on-demand with Athena—10x cheaper.
3. **Right-Sizing Elasticsearch:** If you must use Elasticsearch, ensure hot/warm storage tiers are in place.
4. **Structured Logging:** Store only what matters. Trim noisy debug logs.

A Real-World Example

A SaaS platform I advised had CloudWatch costs balloon from **$500 to $7,000/month** because of forgotten debug logging. One change, setting log retention to 14 days, brought the bill back to $800.

The key insight: Logs are like sandbags. You need them for stability, but keep too many, and they'll sink the boat.

CHAPTER 7

Memory vs. Disk (Or ElastiCache vs. DB)

Our mind is conditioned to "Disk is slow,". But if you're only processing data once every few seconds, and do not need real-time data.

Do you truly need memory-level speed in all areas you are using?

Most companies use REDIS as their dumping bag, and it's a very expensive dumping bag, like a Louie Vuitton bag for storing garbage.

The cost difference between memory-based services (e.g., ElastiCache) and standard databases or disk storage can be stark—memory can be **100x** more expensive. Understand the performance requirements of each component before defaulting to an in-memory solution.

Even for queues, if your read-write requirement is not in 1000s / sec, prefer disk-based queuing like RabbitMQ over RAM-based queuing like REDIS Queue.

In some cases, a hybrid approach, where things are stored in memory but transferred to disk if not processed instantly, saves loads and loads of money. It can be designed after carefully studying your actual use case.

Speed is addictive. Developers love in-memory caching because it makes apps feel blazing fast. But the bill for that speed? Painful.

ElastiCache (Redis/Memcached) can be **100x more expensive** than RDS or disk-based solutions. The problem is when businesses use Redis as a "dumping bag" for everything, not just hot data.

When to Use Memory

- Repeated queries that need sub-millisecond response.
- Session stores for high-traffic apps.
- Real-time leaderboards, gaming scores, or chat applications.

When NOT to Use Memory

- Long-tail analytics queries.
- Low-traffic APIs.
- Queue systems that don't require instant reads/writes.

Cost-Smart Strategies

1. **Hybrid Cache Strategy:** Store hot data in Redis, warm/cold data in RDS/DynamoDB.
2. **Right-Sizing Cache Nodes:** Many companies over-allocate cache clusters "just in case." Start small, monitor hit ratios, and scale only when necessary.
3. **TTL (Time-to-Live):** Use expiration wisely. Don't keep data cached forever if it's rarely used.

A Real-World Example

One ecommerce startup I worked with was using Redis for **everything**, including historical order lookups. Their cache bill alone was **$9,000/month**. By shifting order history to Aurora and keeping only 7-day data in Redis, they cut costs to $1,500/month, with zero customer impact.

Lesson: Treat memory as a *Ferrari*. It's fast, sleek, and powerful, but not your daily grocery car.

CHAPTER 8

Sleep at Night!

Another commonly overlooked area is unused capacity at night, or whenever your user base is off-peak. Your development and staging environments often run at full throttle 24/7, even though no one is actively working on them. Why pay for that? Use AWS features like auto-scaling or scripts that spin down non-critical environments during off-hours.

All this happens automatically, and you save your $$ when you are asleep!

Most infrastructure runs 24/7, even when nobody's using it. Development servers, staging environments, and even certain customer-facing workloads sit idle during nights or weekends. Yet you still pay full price.

The Problem

- Dev/QA servers running all night.
- Analytics clusters crunching nothing at 3 AM.
- Teams are forgetting to shut down temporary test environments.

Solutions

1. **Automated Scheduling:** Use AWS Instance Scheduler or Lambda functions to shut down non-prod environments during off-hours.

   Example: Stop dev servers from 8 PM to 8 AM, saving ~60% instantly.

2. **On-Demand Analytics:** Instead of keeping Redshift or EMR clusters running, spin them up only when needed.

3. **Auto Scaling + Rightsizing:** Let workloads scale down at night with zero manual intervention.

A Real-World Example

A startup in New York had a dev environment of **20 EC2 servers** running 24/7. By applying an auto-shutdown script that turned them off from 9 PM to 7 AM, they saved **$6,500/month,** money that went straight into developer salaries.

Key insight: The cheapest server is the one that's turned off.

CHAPTER 9

"Keep It Under One Roof"

Data traveling across the open internet for internal processes is both costly and risky. By keeping your data transfers "under one roof, i.e., inside the same VPC or through private interconnects, you reduce data egress fees and minimize security exposure. Think of it as hosting a private family gathering instead of dining out at the city's most expensive restaurant every night.

Data transfer costs are the "silent killer" of AWS bills. While storage and compute often get the spotlight, **data egress charges,** traffic leaving AWS or moving between regions, can quietly drain thousands of dollars.

The Mistakes

- EC2s talking over the internet instead of VPC.
- Services in different regions communicate constantly.
- Hybrid setups are moving massive amounts of data out of AWS unnecessarily.

Strategies

1. **Use VPC Endpoints:** Keep traffic private inside AWS instead of paying internet rates.
2. **Keep It Regional:** Minimize cross-region communication unless absolutely necessary.
3. **CloudFront for Distribution:** For customer-facing assets, use CloudFront to cut data transfer costs and latency.

4. **Consolidate Accounts:** Sometimes, costs spiral because multiple AWS accounts are talking to each other inefficiently.

A Real-World Example

One SaaS client had EC2 instances in **us-east-1** constantly querying an RDS in **us-west-2**. That simple misconfiguration led to **$3,000/month in egress charges**. By moving everything under one VPC in a single region, they eliminated the cost completely.

Think of AWS like a big house:

- In-house conversations are free.
- Shouting across the street (cross-region traffic) costs money.
- Sending messages outside the neighborhood (egress to the internet) is the most expensive.

Keeping things "under one roof" is not just about cost; it's also about security, reduced latency, and cleaner architecture.

CHAPTER 10

“Containerization & Kubernetes”

Containerization

Ever heard from your devs: “But it was running perfectly on my machine”? What if we could copy the exact settings, OS settings, and third-party libraries of your dev’s machine and paste them on the server? No more missing libraries, no more lengthy deployment, just ONE readymade black box, ready to deploy. That exact stuff we call a Docker container. It encapsulates whatever is needed to make your service run in a box, which is READY to deploy.

Containerization itself is a powerful tool, but when combined with a manager who can copy the box, arrange multiple boxes into servers, check each box for its working, overload, and manage things for you on the fly, then nothing like it.

Kubernetes does it for you.

To understand more deeply, let’s look at our normal deployments. One EC2 (server) for every workload/service you have. And an overprovisioning of 60-70% on every service, just in case.

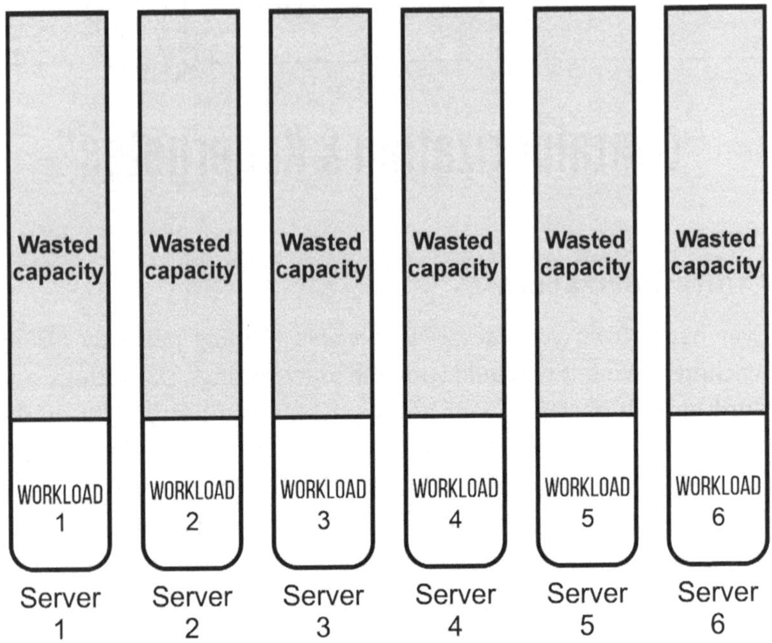

Here, out of the 6 servers, you are effectively using the power of 2 servers, and wasting more than 66% capacity.

So, let's separate the WORKLOAD from the computing capacity.

If you combine all 6 servers into a single pool, would you still need to have that 66% reserve for EVERY server?

Would an extra server be sufficient to handle all spikes? Let's look at the second picture below, where the same ***workload fits neatly in 2 servers, and we have an extra one for JUST IN CASE***. We still have 3 free servers with the same capacity, faster scaling, and auto-healing, just like a full-time DevOps guy managing things for us.

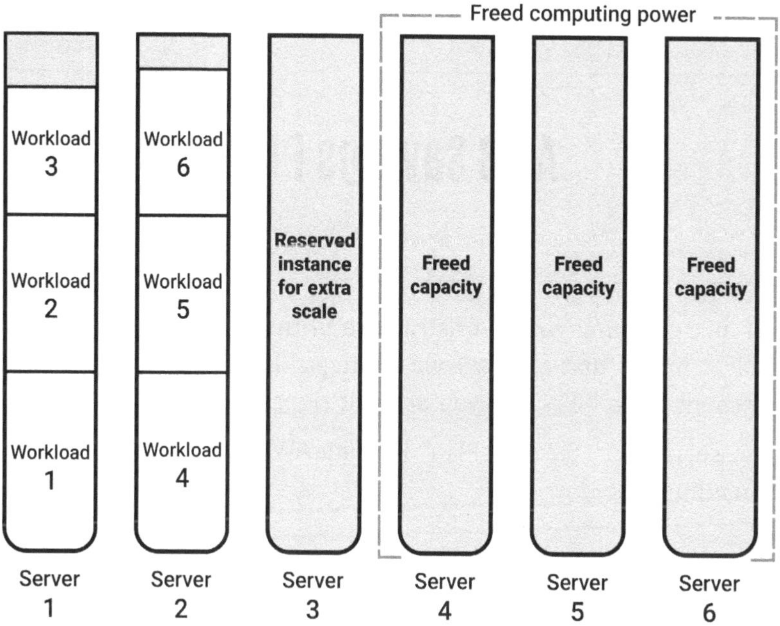

That, ladies and gentlemen, is the power of Kubernetes. It is a powerful, powerful tool to scale worry-free and a must-have for any modern deployment setup, in my opinion.

CHAPTER 11

AWS Savings Plan

This is probably the easiest way to save costs. If you are sure you are not changing your infrastructure in the next 3-6 months or a year, commit that to AWS via Savings Plan, and get an instant discount up to 70%. Yes, you heard it right.

Just search for "Savings Plan" in your AWS console, and you get something like this:

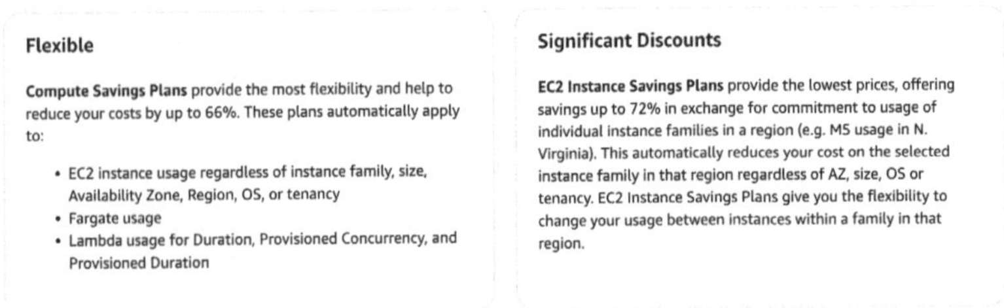

Flexible

Compute Savings Plans provide the most flexibility and help to reduce your costs by up to 66%. These plans automatically apply to:

- EC2 instance usage regardless of instance family, size, Availability Zone, Region, OS, or tenancy
- Fargate usage
- Lambda usage for Duration, Provisioned Concurrency, and Provisioned Duration

Significant Discounts

EC2 Instance Savings Plans provide the lowest prices, offering savings up to 72% in exchange for commitment to usage of individual instance families in a region (e.g. M5 usage in N. Virginia). This automatically reduces your cost on the selected instance family in that region regardless of AZ, size, OS or tenancy. EC2 Instance Savings Plans give you the flexibility to change your usage between instances within a family in that region.

Committing to a particular instance type gives maximum savings in the tune of 70%.

Spot Instances

If you are already on Auto Scaling, try ***spot instances***. (instead of on-demand)

Think of it as **renting a car daily (on-demand)** vs **booking last-minute cancellations for way cheaper (spot)**.

Spot instances are instances that are not actively being used by the person to whom its allocated and are available way cheaper (Up to **90% cheaper)** than On-Demand instances (the ones you are using).

One drawback to these is that AWS may take it back from you on a minute's notice. But it doesn't matter, let's say for an API service.

A good strategy is to have your base instance in an Auto Scaling setup to be on-demand, and the additional resources as Spot Instances. Please do not use Spot instances in areas where a sudden going down of a service can affect stability, eg, a long-standing operation of 1 hour. Use it in services that are interrupt-tolerant and stateless, like ETL Jobs, Video Rendering, Performance Analysis, APIs, Dev Test Envs, etc.

CHAPTER 12

Additional Insight and Real-World Examples

Let's look at a few more cases that highlight how small misconfigurations can lead to big bills:

1. **$30,000 CloudFront Cost Example**

   A large e-commerce store in London faced a sudden, staggering CloudFront bill due to a misconfigured invalidation process stuck in a loop. This type of programming error bills could have been easily avoided by setting up AWS Budgets alarms.

2. **Redundant EKS/MySQL Cost**

   One client kept a "backup" EKS cluster and MySQL server running 24/7, each with a full production-grade setup. By shifting to on-demand backups and an on-call replica, they halved their monthly AWS bill.

These examples prove that AWS cost issues are not always about "lack of money." They're about *lack of awareness* and *unnecessary duplication*.

CHAPTER 13

Common Mind Blocks & How to Overcome Them

1. **"We don't have time to optimize; we're busy shipping new features."**

   Answer: Costly overhead slows you down in the long run. Spend a fraction of the time now to free up budget for more critical areas of development.

2. **"We're worried about performance hitting rock bottom if we cut resources."**

   Answer: True optimization pinpoints *unnecessary* resources, not critical ones. Often, cleaning up yields performance *improvements* because the system becomes leaner and more efficient.

3. **"We don't have a complete map of our infrastructure."**

   Answer: The process of cost review helps you *create* that map. You'll gain better visibility while cutting costs.

4. **"It might break something, and we don't know what!"**

   Answer: Use the "Control-Alt-Delete" approach—test, rename, archive, wait. With a systematic procedure, real-time breakage risks are minimal.

CHAPTER 14

Summarizing the Key Takeaways & Next Steps

- **Overprovisioning** is often driven by fear.
- **Redundant data** and **redundant logs** accumulate quietly, inflating bills.
- **Memory vs. Disk**: Choose wisely based on your performance needs.
- **Lifecycle policies** for data and logs can drastically cut costs.
- **Nightly & off-peak optimization** can save you a bundle.
- **In-house data transfers** are cheaper and more secure than public data transfers.
- **Regular 3-month reviews** will reveal new layers of insight into your system's usage patterns and potential for savings.

By now, you've seen how cutting AWS costs doesn't just help your budget; it sharpens your entire operation. You can absolutely tackle these optimizations yourself, no question. Yet it can be a tricky, time-intensive process. For many teams, spending weeks or months figuring out every nuance can be overwhelming.

- I'm confident that you *can* do all this on your own. If you have the time and the right mindset, go forth and conquer—your AWS bill will thank you, and you'll sleep better knowing you're running a lean, efficient infrastructure.
- But if you'd prefer a helping hand to make your journey speedier and smoother, me and my team of rockstar DevOps professionals are only a message away. Check with us to see if we can help

you accelerate the journey, spot hidden costs, and automate your cost savings routine.

Drop us a WhatsApp at +91 80507 33372 with the message: "Help me save our AWS Cost!"

Or if email is more your style, reach out at: **letsoptimize@thecloudguy.ai**

Whichever path you choose, you've already taken the first step by arming yourself with the knowledge in this book. Now, take action, start trimming those unnecessary expenses, and enjoy the freedom of a smoother, more cost-effective AWS experience.

Thank you for joining me on this journey. Until next time, may your logs be short, your bills be small, and your success be greater than ever before!